UKRAINE

Big Buddy Books
An Imprint of Abdo Publishing
abdopublishing.com

Julie Murray

abdopublishing.com

Published by Abdo Publishing, a division of ABDO, PO Box 398166, Minneapolis, Minnesota 55439.
Copyright © 2018 by Abdo Consulting Group, Inc. International copyrights reserved in all countries. No part
of this book may be reproduced in any form without written permission from the publisher. Big Buddy Books™
is a trademark and logo of Abdo Publishing.

Printed in the United States of America, North Mankato, Minnesota.
052017
092017

Cover Photo: Shutterstock.com.
Interior Photos: Agencja Fotograficzna Caro/Alamy Stock Photo (p. 19); Kosmenko Dmytro/Alamy Stock
    Photo (p. 38); Dino Fracchia/Alamy Stock Photo (p. 34); ©iStockphoto.com (pp. 5, 9, 11, 15, 17, 21, 25,
    35); Maskot/Alamy Stock Photo (p. 27); Oleksandr Prykhodko/Alamy Stock Photo (p. 34); REUTERS/
    Alamy Stock Photo (pp. 19, 31, 33); Shutterstock (p. 37); Suddeutsche Zeitung/Granger, NYC — All rights
    reserved. (p. 13); Mikhail Tolstoy/Alamy Stock Photo (p. 29); Ivan Vdovin/Alamy Stock Photo (p. 16);
    Oleksiy Yakovlyev/Alamy Stock Photo (p. 23); YAY Media AS/Alamy Stock Photo (p. 23); Zoonar GmbH/
    Alamy Stock Photo (p. 11).

Coordinating Series Editor: Tamara L. Britton
Editor: Katie Lajiness
Graphic Design: Taylor Higgins, Keely McKernan

Country population and area figures taken from the CIA World Factbook.

Publisher's Cataloging-in-Publication Data

Names: Murray, Julie, 1969- , author.
Title: Ukraine / by Julie Murray.
Description: Minneapolis, MN : Abdo Publishing, 2018. | Series: Explore the
    countries | Includes bibliographical references and index.
Identifiers: LCCN 2016962354 | ISBN 9781532110535 (lib. bdg.) |
    ISBN 9781680788389 (ebook)
Subjects: LCSH: Ukraine--Juvenile literature.
Classification: DDC 947.7--dc23
LC record available at http://lccn.loc.gov/2016962354

UKRAINE

CONTENTS

AROUND THE WORLD

Our world has many countries. Each country has beautiful land. It has its own rich history. And, the people have their own languages and ways of life.

Ukraine is a country in Europe. What do you know about Ukraine? Let's learn more about this place and its story!

Did You Know?

Ukrainian is the country's official language.

The Potemkin Stairway is one of Odessa's most popular spots. It has 192 stairs leading down to the port of Odessa.

SAY IT

Ukraine
YOO-krayn

Passport to Ukraine

Ukraine is a country in Eastern Europe. It shares borders with seven countries. The Black Sea and the Sea of Azov are to the south.

The country's total area is about 233,032 square miles (603,550 sq km). More than 44 million people live there.

Did You Know?

Ukraine is slightly smaller than the state of Texas.

WHERE IN THE WORLD?

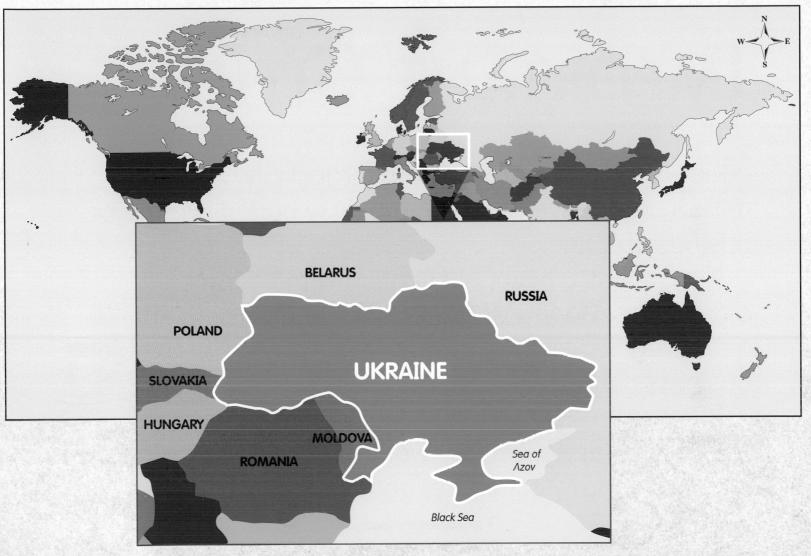

IMPORTANT CITIES

Kiev is Ukraine's **capital** and largest city. Almost 3 million people live there. With a busy port, it is a major business center.

The city has a history of fighting with **Vikings** and other tribes. During **World War II**, German soldiers destroyed the city. But over time, Kiev became a major business center.

Today, many people in Kiev work in government or manufacturing. Factory workers make processed foods and many consumer goods.

SAY IT

Kiev
KEE-ehf

UKRAINE

Kiev ★

Kharkiv •

Odessa •

N
W E
S

Kiev has a port on the Dnieper River. The river flows about 1,367 miles (2,200 km) into the Black Sea.

9

With about 1.4 million people, Kharkiv is Ukraine's second-largest city. Three rivers connect near Kharkiv. In the 1650s, Kharkiv was founded as a Russian military outpost. Today, factories there make airplanes and military items. It is also home to the world's largest tractor factory.

Odessa is Ukraine's third-largest city. It is home to more than 1 million people. In 1866, a railway helped the city to grow quickly. After **World War II**, Odessa was in ruins. Today, the city is a manufacturing center. Workers make tools, paints, and processed food.

SAY IT

Kharkiv
KAHR-kuhf

Odessa
oh-DEH-suh

The Blagoveshchensky Cathedral in Kharkiv was completed in 1888.

At the Odessa train station, fast rail trains allow for overnight travel to almost any other place in Ukraine.

UKRAINE IN HISTORY

Throughout history, Ukraine had to fight to rule itself. In the 1300s, Lithuania controlled most of the country. After 1569, Poland took over. In 1648, a group of locals called the Cossacks fought against the Polish. They won and formed a new state.

By the 1700s, Russia was the next country to take over Ukraine. By 1922, Ukraine was part of the **Soviet Union**. Ukrainians were not allowed to own businesses or choose their own jobs. The government took their land and many went hungry.

The Cossacks are a group of military men from Ukraine and Russia. They fought in the trenches during World War I.

In the mid-1920s, a **Communist** leader named Joseph Stalin took control of the **Soviet Union**. He ruled for about 25 years. And, many people died under his command.

During **World War II**, Germany attacked Ukraine. Millions of Ukrainians were killed or forced to work as slaves.

In 1991, the Soviet Union came to an end. Then Ukraine became an independent country. However, the country continued to struggle because of unfair elections.

To honor Ukraine's independence, Kiev's main square was named Independence Square.

TIMELINE

1256

The king of Rus founded the first city in what is now Ukraine.

1608

The University of Lviv was established.

1917–1920

During part of **World War I**, Ukraine briefly became an independent nation.

16

1932–1933

About 7 million people died of hunger under Stalin's rule.

1986

The Chernobyl **nuclear** power station exploded. People, animals, and land were badly hurt.

2015

The leaders of Russia and Ukraine agreed on a peace plan between the two countries.

An Important Symbol

The Ukrainian flag is half blue and half yellow. Blue is for the sky, mountains, and streams. The yellow is for Ukraine's wheat fields.

The Ukrainian government is a **semi-presidential republic**. The government includes a president and a prime minister. The president is the head of state. In Ukraine, the president serves a five-year term. The prime minister is head of government.

The Ukrainian flag was adopted in 1992.

In 2014, Petro Poroshenko was elected president of Ukraine.

In 2016, Volodymyr Groysman became the prime minister. He is Ukraine's youngest prime minister.

SAY IT

Petro Poroshenko
peht-ROH puhr-oh-SHANK-oh

Volodymyr Groysman
vohl-ahd-DUH-mihr GROYS-man

ACROSS THE LAND

Most of Ukraine is very flat. Grass covers much of the central and southern areas. The northern area has one of Europe's largest wetlands.

Ukraine's mountains are in the western part of the country. The highest peak in Ukraine is Mount Hoverla. It is about 6,762 feet (2,061 m) high.

Did You Know?

In January, the average temperature in Kharkiv is about 19°F (–7°C). In July, it is about 68°F (20°C).

The Dnieper River is the fourth longest in Europe.

Ukraine's steppe covers about 89,000 square miles (230,509 sq km). In a steppe, much of the area is covered by grasslands.

Many types of animals live in Ukraine. About 350 different kinds of birds and 200 kinds of fish live there. Ukraine's most common wild animals include elk, foxes, raccoons, and wolves.

Some Kulans live in a nature reserve in Ukraine. They are related to wild donkeys.

A marmot is a rodent that lives in the Ukrainian steppe. While a group feeds, one marmot stands and looks out for danger.

23

Earning a Living

Many Ukrainians work with their hands. In factories, they produce iron, steel, trains, tractors, and other goods. Some people dig deep underground for coal and salt. Farmers raise cows, goats, pigs, and sheep. And, they grow corn, oats, potatoes, and wheat.

Grains are Ukraine's top farm product, followed by sugar beets and sunflower seeds.

LIFE IN UKRAINE

Ukraine has a rich, artistic society. Many cities have ballet companies, theaters, and opera houses. Ukraine is also known for its great writers. During the 1930s, many writers were punished for printing anti-**Communist** work.

In Ukraine, breads and wheat dishes are important parts of many meals. People eat heavy meals with lots of meat and sauces. They also drink many cups of tea.

Did You Know?

In Ukraine, children must attend school from ages 6 to 18. After ninth grade, students choose a general education, trade, or tech school.

Borscht is a popular soup. It is usually made with beets, carrots, potatoes, and spinach.

In Ukraine, people enjoy sports such as basketball, gymnastics, and swimming. However, soccer is the country's most popular sport.

Nearly half of Ukrainians are Eastern Orthodox **Christians**. Many people do not follow any religion. A small group is **Jewish**.

The Cathedral of Saint Sophia is almost 1,000 years old. It is the oldest standing church in Kiev.

FAMOUS FACES

Many talented people live in Ukraine. Yana Klochkova was born on August 7, 1982, in Simferopol, Ukraine. She swam in medley races. From 2000 to 2004, Klochkova lost only one medley race at a world event.

In 2004, Klochkova made Olympic history. She became the first woman to win gold in the same events in two straight games. That year, *Swimming World* magazine named her World Female Swimmer of the Year.

Did You Know?

In a medley race, swimmers use a different stroke for each part of the race.

During the 2004 Olympics, Klochkova won gold in the women's 200-meter individual medley.

SAY IT

Yana Klochkova
YAH-nuh KLOHCH-koh-va

Ruslan Ponomariov was born on October 11, 1983, in Horlivka, Ukraine. He is one of the world's best chess players. At 14, Ponomariov was the youngest player to become a grandmaster. This is the highest title a player can earn.

From 2002 to 2004, he was the World Chess Federation's top player. In 2009, Ponomariov won second place in the World Chess Cup.

SAY IT

Ruslan Ponomariov
roo-SLAWN pawn-NO-mahr-ree-awv

At 18, Ponomariov became the youngest grandmaster to become world chess champion.

TOUR BOOK

Imagine traveling to Ukraine! Here are some places you could go and things you could do.

Imagine

Kiev Academic Puppet Theater is the oldest in Ukraine. Since 1927, this theater has charmed children from around the world.

Remember

The National Chernobyl Museum holds a collection of items related to the **nuclear** explosion.

 Explore

The Odessa Catacombs is the longest system of tunnels in the world. It is more than 1,500 miles (2,414 km) long.

Seek

Built in 1912, Swallow's Nest is a castle overlooking the Black Sea. The castle has been in some Ukrainian movies.

 Discover

The Tunnel of Love is a popular spot for people to make a wish. Walk this tree-lined tunnel created by a train.

A GREAT COUNTRY

The story of Ukraine is important to our world. Ukraine is a land of mountains and grasslands. It is a country of hardworking people.

The people and places that make up Ukraine offer something special. They help make the world a more beautiful, interesting place.

The Bell of Chersonesos is near the Black Sea. Ukraine and Russia often fight over who controls this land.

Ukraine Up Close

Official Name: Ukraine

Flag:

Population (rank): 44,209,733
(July 2016 est.)
(32nd most-populated country)

Total Area (rank): 233,032 square miles
(46th largest country)

Capital: Kiev

Official Language: Ukrainian

Currency: Ukrainian hryvnia

Form of Government: Semi-presidential
republic

National Anthem:"Shche ne vmerla
Ukraina" ("Ukraine Has Not Yet Died")

IMPORTANT WORDS

capital a city where government leaders meet.

Christian (KRIHS-chuhn) a person who practices Christianity, which is a religion that follows the teachings of Jesus Christ.

Communist (KAHM-yuh-nihst) of or relating to a form of government in which all or most land and goods are owned by the state. They are then divided among the people based on need.

Jewish a person who practices Judaism, which is a religion based on laws recorded in the Torah, or is related to the ancient Hebrews.

nuclear a type of energy that uses atoms. Atoms are tiny particles that make up matter.

semi-presidential republic a form of government in which an elected president shares power with a prime minister and an elected legislature.

Soviet Union the first country to form a government based on the system known as Communism. It existed from 1922 to 1991.

Vikings one of the Scandinavians who raided or invaded the coast of Europe from the 700s to the 900s.

World War I a war fought in Europe from 1914 to 1918.

World War II a war fought in Europe, Asia, and Africa from 1939 to 1945.

WEBSITES

To learn more about Explore the Countries, visit **abdobooklinks.com**. These links are routinely monitored and updated to provide the most current information available.

INDEX